SCIENCE FACTORY
AIR AND FLIGHT

JON RICHARDS

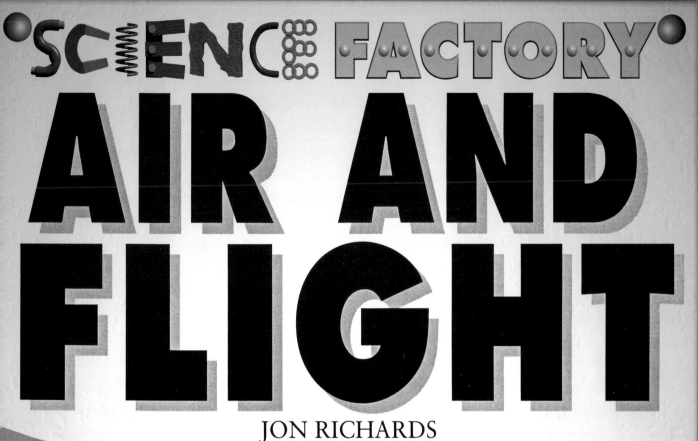

COPPER BEECH BOOKS
BROOKFIELD, CONNECTICUT

© Aladdin Books Ltd 1999

Designed and produced by
Aladdin Books Ltd
28 Percy Street
London W1P 0LD

First published in the United States
in 1999 by
Copper Beech Books,
an imprint of
The Millbrook Press
2 Old New Milford Road
Brookfield, Connecticut

Design
David West
Children's Book Design

Designer
Flick Killerby

Illustrator
Ian Thompson

Printed in Belgium

Some of the illustrations in this series
have appeared in previous books
published by Aladdin Books.

All the photos in this book were
taken by Roger Vlitos.

Cataloging-in-Publication Data is on
file at the Library of Congress.

ISBN 0-7613-0918-7 (lib. bdg.)

5 4 3 2 1

INTRODUCTION

You can't see it, but air is one of the most important things in your life. It is made up of a mixture of gases that lie around the earth in a layer called the atmosphere. Not only do you breathe air in to keep you alive, but it is used to push boats, and it can even help planes to fly through the sky. Read on and discover a host of experiments, as well as the "why-it-works" boxes, which will teach you more about the power of air!

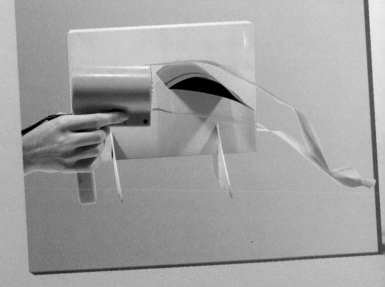

CONTENTS

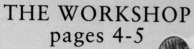

THE WORKSHOP

BEFORE YOU START any of the experiments, it is important that you learn a few simple rules about the care of your science factory.

● Always keep your hands and the work surfaces clean. Dirt can damage results and ruin an experiment!

● Read the instructions carefully before you start each experiment.

● Make sure you have all the equipment you need for the experiment (see checklist opposite).

● If you don't have the right piece of equipment, then improvise. For example, a liquid soap bottle will do just as well as a plastic drinks bottle.

● Don't be afraid to make mistakes. Just start again — patience is very important!

Equipment checklist:
- Scissors, tape, and glue
- Hair dryer
- Plastic bottles and fruit-juice cartons
- Glass jars and cardboard boxes
- Ping-Pong balls
- Toy cars
- Paper, cardboard, and tissue paper
- Modeling clay
- Ribbons
- Aluminum foil
- Wire
- Ballpoint pens
- Drinking straws and balloons
- Plastic cups and tubs
- Toothpicks, sticks, and matchsticks
- Cotton thread
- Rubber bands

WARNING:

Some of the experiments in this book need the help of an adult. Always ask a grown-up to give you a hand when you are using scissors or electrical objects such as hair dryers!

GOING UP

WHAT YOU
NEED
Aluminum foil
Thin
cardboard
Cotton thread
Modeling clay
Tape
Stick

WINDS AND WEATHER ON THE EARTH ARE CAUSED BY DIFFERENCES IN AIR TEMPERATURE. Heat from the sun warms the ground in one spot, which, in turn, warms the air just above it. As this air is warmed, it expands, becoming lighter or less dense. This less dense air rises, forming air currents, or winds. You can copy and see these air movements on a smaller scale using some foil shapes and a heater.

Watch as your aluminum foil shapes twirl in the warm air rising from the heater.

MOBILE AIR

1 Cut some strips of aluminum foil into shapes.

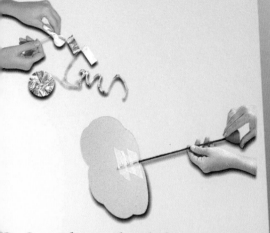

2 Attach a length of cotton thread to each foil shape.

3 Cut a large cloud shape out of cardboard, fix it to a stick, and secure a piece of modeling clay to the base. Make sure that it will stand up.

4 Attach the foil shapes to the cardboard cloud and place your mobile above a heater — keep it away from any flames.

WHY IT WORKS

Air above the heater is warmed, becomes less dense, and starts to rise. This rising warm air pushes against your foil shapes, causing them to turn.

DIRECTION OF MOVEMENT

ALUMINUM SHAPES DEFLECTED BY WARM AIR

ALUMINUM SHAPES

RISING WARM AIR

ALL SHAPES AND SIZES

See how well some other foil shapes spin. You will find that some shapes spin better because they are deflected more easily by the rising warm air.

TWISTED LOOP

CURVE

HOT-AIR BALLOON

BECAUSE HOT AIR RISES (SEE PAGES 6-7), it can be used to lift things into the air. For more than 200 years, people have flown through the air in hot-air balloons. The first hot-air balloon was built in 1783 by two French brothers, Joseph and Jaques Montgolfier. This experiment shows how to build your own miniature hot-air balloon and how it can fly.

WHAT YOU NEED
Tissue paper
Glue
Cardboard
Cotton thread
Hair dryer

UP, UP, AND AWAY

1 *Fold a sheet of tissue paper in half and cut out one panel for your hot-air balloon.*

2 *Repeat this using different colors of tissue paper, until you have cut out four panels.*

3 Glue the edges of your panels together to make your balloon.

4 Fold a piece of cardboard to make a small basket and attach it to the bottom of your balloon using four lengths of cotton thread.

WHY IT WORKS

WARM AIR INSIDE THE BALLOON

The air inside your balloon is warmer and less dense than the air outside it. As a result, this air inside the balloon rises, carrying the balloon up with it.

5 Blow the balloon up with hot air from a hair dryer. Watch it rise from the ground.

GETTING HEAVY

Make some figures out of modeling clay and place them inside the balloon's basket. You will find that the more weight the balloon has to carry, the harder it will be to fly.

SAILING AWAY

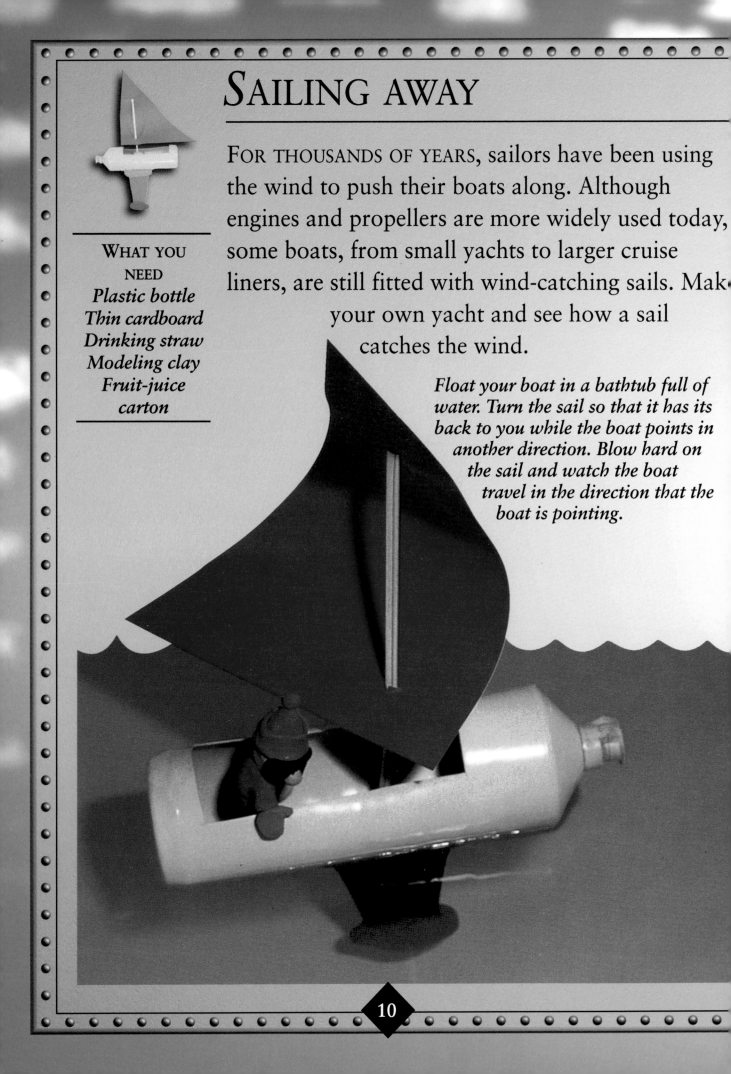

FOR THOUSANDS OF YEARS, sailors have been using the wind to push their boats along. Although engines and propellers are more widely used today, some boats, from small yachts to larger cruise liners, are still fitted with wind-catching sails. Make your own yacht and see how a sail catches the wind.

WHAT YOU NEED
Plastic bottle
Thin cardboard
Drinking straw
Modeling clay
Fruit-juice carton

Float your boat in a bathtub full of water. Turn the sail so that it has its back to you while the boat points in another direction. Blow hard on the sail and watch the boat travel in the direction that the boat is pointing.

SAIL POWER

1 Cut a rectangular piece out of the side of a plastic bottle to make your boat's body.

2 Fix a lump of modeling clay in the bottom of your boat and use it to hold a straw mast.

3 Cut a triangular piece of paper to make a sail and pierce two holes in it to thread your mast through.

4 Cut out a wedge-shaped piece from a fruit-juice carton — this will be your keel. Fix a lump of modeling clay to each end and stick the keel to the boat's bottom.

WHY IT WORKS

As the wind catches the sail it tries to push the boat sideways. However, the resistance of the water on the keel stops the boat from going sideways. Instead the boat is pushed forward.

DIRECTION OF BOAT'S TRAVEL

SAIL

DIRECTION OF WIND

KEEL

WATER RESISTANCE

MOVING YOUR SAILS

Try moving the position of your sail. You will find that the boat moves with less control when the sail is not above the keel.

SAIL FIXED AT FRONT

SAIL FIXED AT REAR

TELLING THE WEATHER

WHAT YOU NEED
Glass jar
Thin cardboard
Drinking straw
Toothpick
Balloon
Rubber band

EVEN THOUGH YOU CAN'T SEE IT, air has weight. The tiny molecules that make up air are attracted to the earth by gravity, making them press on you. This is called air pressure. Air pressure is changing all the time, as air currents move over the planet and the weather changes. You can make a device that measures these changes in air pressure — it's called a barometer.

RAIN OR SHINE?

1 Cut the neck off a balloon and stretch the balloon over a glass jar. Secure the balloon with a rubber band.

2 Tape a toothpick to the end of a straw and tape the other end of the straw to the center of the balloon lid.

3 Fold a sheet of cardboard and fix a card triangle to the back to support it. Fix a pressure chart in place showing good weather at the top and bad weather at the bottom.

FEEL THE PRESSURE

Try to lever up some paper using a ruler. Air pressure on the paper will make this quite hard. You can see the weight of air by balancing two full balloons, then emptying one.

— AIR PRESSURE

FORCE

FULL BALLOON

EMPTY BALLOON

4 Put the barometer in front of the chart and mark where the pointer moves up and down over a few days.

WHY IT WORKS

Changes in air pressure will cause the balloon lid to bend, moving the pointer. A rise in air pressure is a sign of good weather, and a fall in air pressure is a sign of bad weather.

HIGHER AIR PRESSURE PUSHES DOWN ON THE BALLOON

POINTER RISES

POINTER FALLS

LOWER AIR PRESSURE CAUSES THE BALLOON TO BEND OUT

FALLING PRESSURE

HAVE YOU NOTICED HOW FAST-MOVING OBJECTS, such as cars and trains, seem to pull objects after them when they race by? This is because these fast object push air along quickly. As the objects push air along, they create low pressure behind them, and air from around the sides is sucked in to equal out the difference in pressure. You can see this effect in action with this phenomenon.

WHAT YOU NEED
Two Ping-Pong balls
Two straws
Modeling clay
Hair dryer

BLOWING BALLS

1 *Stick small lumps of modeling clay to the ends of two drinking straws. The best straws to use are the flexible type with the crinkled section.*

2 *Attach Ping-Pong balls onto the modeling clay at the ends of the straws farthest from the crinkled section. Stick the other ends of the straws onto a flat surface, making sure that the straws can stand up.*

AIR SQUEEZE

Blow between two sheets of paper. The low air pressure created by your blowing causes the sheets to come together.

3 *Blow downward onto the balls using a hair dryer and watch as the two balls move toward each other.*

WHY IT WORKS

The fast-moving air flowing between the two balls creates an area of low pressure between the balls. The balls are then pushed together by higher air pressure outside them.

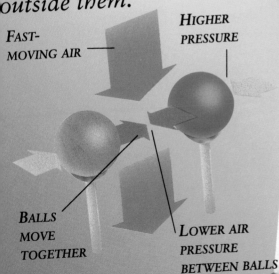

FAST-MOVING AIR

HIGHER PRESSURE

BALLS MOVE TOGETHER

LOWER AIR PRESSURE BETWEEN BALLS

RISING PAPER

Blow over the surface of a piece of paper held by your mouth. The air you blow out creates an area of low air pressure above the paper, which causes the paper to rise.

FLOATING ON AIR

SOME VEHICLES, SUCH AS THE HOVERCRAFT, travel on top of a cushion of air. This removes any friction between the vehicle and the surface. Friction is a force between surfaces that can slow a vehicle down, making it harder for it to move. Build your own hovercraft and see how it moves about with little effort.

WHAT YOU NEED

Plastic tub
Hair dryer

SPEEDY HOVERCRAFT

1 *Take a clean, light-weight plastic tub and cut a hole in its base — this will be your hovercraft. Decorate the hovercraft as you like.*

2 *Place your hovercraft on a smooth surface. Blow air from a hair dryer into the hole and watch as your hovercraft starts to float on a cushion of air. Now try pushing your hovercraft — notice how easily it glides around.*

ADDING TO THE WEIGHT

Try adding some coins to the top of your hovercraft and see how this affects its movement. You will find that the heavier your hovercraft becomes, the more air is needed to lift it, and the harder it becomes for it to move about.

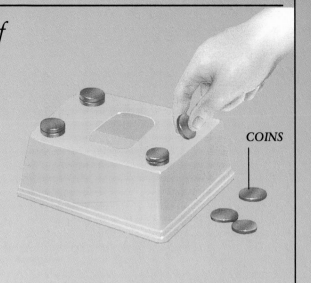

COINS

WHY IT WORKS

As the hovercraft rises on a cushion of air, it no longer rubs against the surface. There is no longer any friction between the hovercraft and the surface, and the hovercraft can move easily.

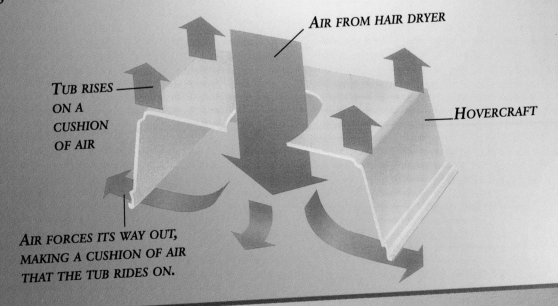

AIR FROM HAIR DRYER

TUB RISES ON A CUSHION OF AIR

HOVERCRAFT

AIR FORCES ITS WAY OUT, MAKING A CUSHION OF AIR THAT THE TUB RIDES ON.

Sharp shape

What you need
Two identical toy cars
Thin cardboard
Tape
Hair dryer

HAVE YOU NOTICED THAT FAST RACING CARS ARE VER POINTED? This streamlined shape lets them move through the air more easily and quickly. On the other hand, objects with an unstreamlined shape can be slowed down as they travel through the air. These experiments will show you how an object's shape can affect its movement.

The car covered by the curved cardboard will experience less air resistance and will travel down the ramp faster than the other car.

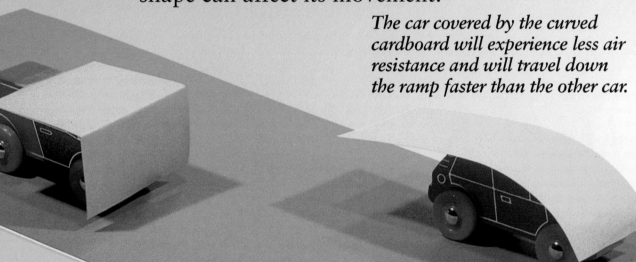

SLOWING THE FALL

Make a parachute by tying some cotton thread to four corners of a handkerchief. Fix a lump of modeling clay to the other ends of the cotton thread and throw it in the air. The parachute slows its fall because it traps air molecules under it, creating air resistance.

WHY IT WORKS

The car with the curved cardboard travels faster because its shape disturbs the air less. The car with the unstreamlined body disturbs the air. This disturbed air increases the force called drag, which slows the car down.

AIR MOVES OVER EASILY

DRAG

SQUARED FRONT

STREAMLINED SHAPE

DISTURBED AIR

STREAMLINED SHAPES

1 Take two identical model cars. Make sure that each moves as easily as the other. Cut out cardboard rectangles that will cover the cars.

2 Attach the rectangles to the front of the cars. Fold one smoothly over the top to form a curve and bend the other one to form a right angle.

3 Tilt a board on a book to form a ramp. Release the cars from the top of the ramp at the same time into a wind caused by the hair dryer.

TESTING TIME

WHAT YOU
NEED
Cardboard
box
Sticks
Ribbons
Hair dryer

WHEN DESIGNERS ARE TESTING THE SHAPES OF NEW CARS, planes, and rockets, they use wind tunnels to see how air will pass over the shapes. Trails of smoke are blown over the objects to show this mor[e] easily. Build your own wind tunnel and test the shapes of different objects.

WIND TUNNEL

1 *Make a backdrop for your wind tunnel using a cardboard box and two triangular bases.*

2 *Cut slits in the base of the box and slide the two bases in to hold the box upright.*

3 *Carefully make hole[s] in the center of the box and push two thin sticks through them. These sticks will support objects tha[t] you are testing in your wind tunnel.*

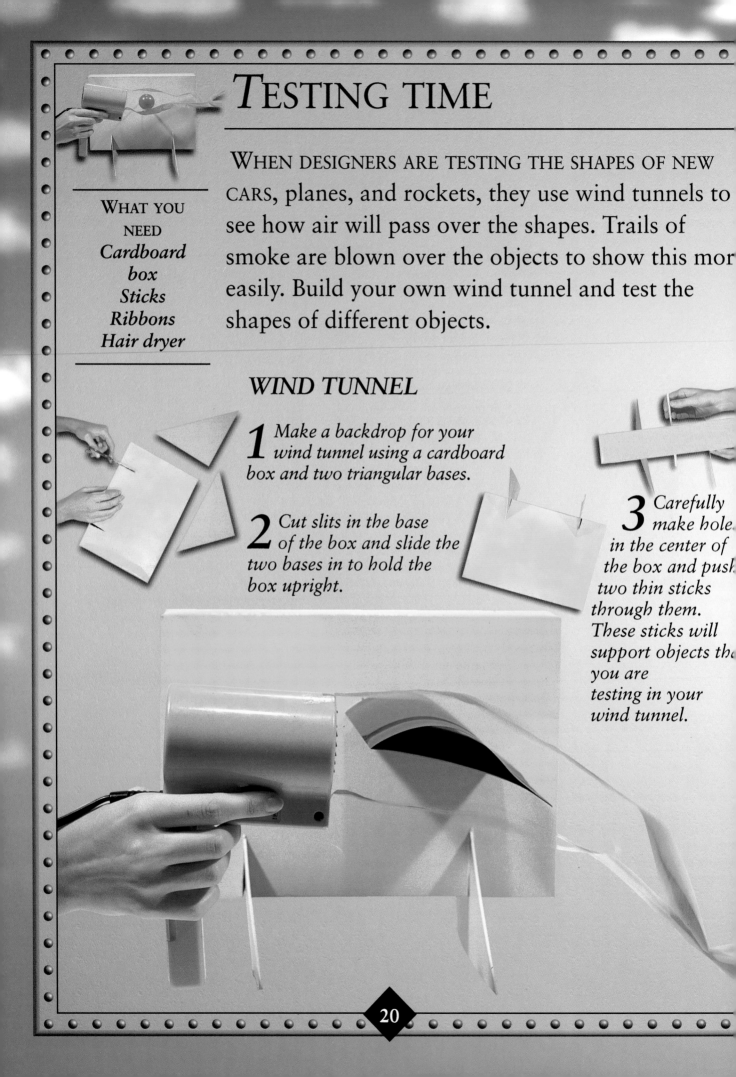

TESTING TIME

See how the two cars you used in the experiment on pages 18-19 test out in your wind tunnel.

4 *Fix two ribbons to each side of a hair dryer. With the dryer on "cool" setting, watch how the ribbons blow over a number of objects, such as a wing section (airfoil — see pages 22-23) and a ball.*

WHY IT WORKS

The air will pass over streamlined objects easily without causing much drag (see pages 18-19). However, unstreamlined shapes, such as the ball, will disturb the air flow, making the ribbons flap around.

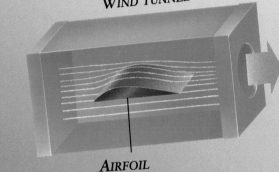

WIND TUNNEL

AIRFOIL

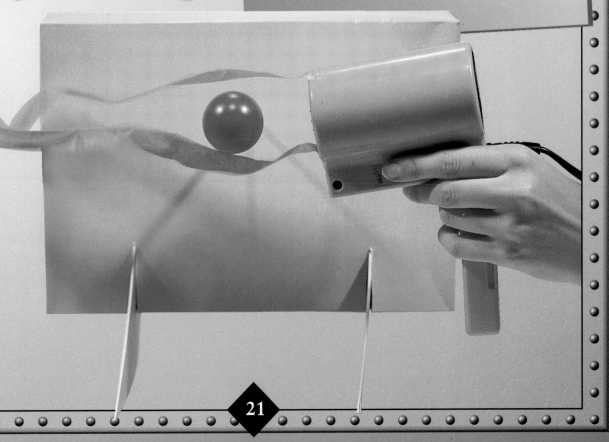

FLYING WINGS

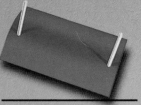

WHAT YOU NEED
Thin cardboard
Tape
Two straws
Cotton thread
Hair dryer

BIRDS AND AIRCRAFT STAY IN THE AIR BECAUSE OF THE SHAPE OF THEIR WINGS. This special shape is called an airfoil. An airfoil is flat on the bottom and curved on the top. This experiment will show you how this shape causes a wing to rise as air passes over it.

AIRFOIL

1 Fold a rectangular piece of cardboard in two, leaving a slight overlap.

2 Push the overlapping ends together so that one side of the folded cardboard is now curved.

3 Tape the ends of the cardboard together to form your wing. Ask an adult to pierce holes at either end of your wing, using a knitting needle or a sharp pencil.

4 Now push a drinking straw through each pair of holes.

5 Pass lengths of cotton thread through each straw and pull them tight. Make sure the curved edge of your wing is on top.

6 Lift the wing a little and aim a hairdryer at the folded edge. Turn on the hairdryer, release the wing and watch it rise.

WHY IT WORKS

Because the wing is curved on top and flat underneath, air flowing over the wing has farther to travel — so it has to flow faster. Faster-flowing air has less pressure (see pages 14-15). The higher pressure below the wing then pushes the wing up.

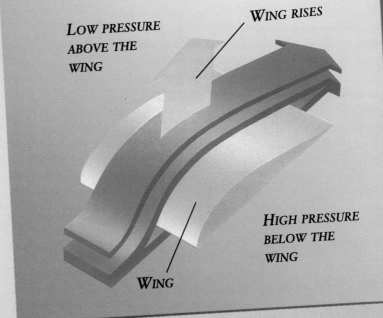

LOW PRESSURE ABOVE THE WING

WING RISES

WING

HIGH PRESSURE BELOW THE WING

BIGGER WINGS

Move the hairdryer away from the wing. The wing will not rise as easily.

LARGER AIRFOIL

FIRST AIRFOIL

You can also make a wing with a larger curved surface. This new wing will rise more easily because it creates more lift.

CONTROLLED FLIGHT

BIRDS AND AIRCRAFT CAN FLY IN A CONTROLLED WAY because they have movable surfaces. Birds use their wings and tail feathers, while aircraft have flaps. Build your own glider and see how these movable surfaces can affect the flight of your aircraft.

ROLL, PITCH, AND YAW

Make your glider roll by moving the flaps on the wings. You can make your glider climb or dive (called pitch) by moving the flaps on the horizontal part of the tailplane. Make your glider move from side to side (yaw) by moving the flap on the upright part of the tailplane.

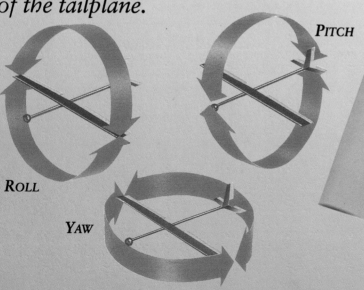

PITCH

ROLL

YAW

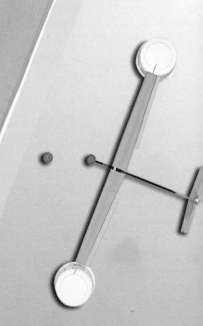

WHY IT WORKS

The lift created by the shape of the wings makes your glider fly. The movable surfaces turn the glider by deflecting the air as it flows over them. This deflected air pushes against the movable surfaces with enough force to alter the glider's course.

GLIDE AWAY

1 Cut out your wings and tailplane from cardboard in the shapes shown. Cut out some thin strips of cardboard, which will be stuck to the wings and the tailplane. These will make the movable surfaces.

2 Fold the wings over and tape together to make an airfoil shape (see pages 22-23). Feed a drinking straw through the wing to keep its airfoil shape. Fold the tailplane into shape so that it looks like a T when seen from the front.

3 Stick the thin strips of cardboard in place on the back of each wing and also on the back of all three parts of the tailplane. Stick the wing on a thin stick, which will act as the glider's body. Attach the tailplane to a piece of a drinking straw and tape this onto the back of the stick.

4 Your glider should balance if it is rested on two cups by its wings. Add a lump of modeling clay to your glider's nose and change the amount until the glider balances evenly. Now you can fly your glider.

USING THE WIND

WHAT YOU NEED
Drinks carton
Drinking straws
Thin cardboard
Wire
Ballpoint pen
Modeling clay

WINDS CAN BLOW VERY STRONGLY. Hurricanes have caused lots of damage, uprooting trees and even demolishing houses! But winds can also be helpful. For hundreds of years, people have used the wind as a source of power to pump water up from deep well or to grind wheat into flour. This experiment shows you how to build your own windmill and how it car harness the power of the wind.

WORKING WINDMILL

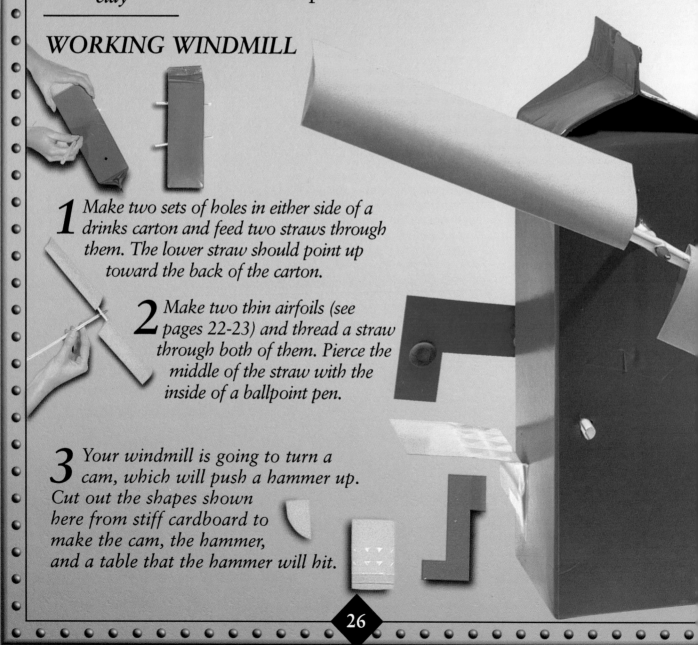

1 Make two sets of holes in either side of a drinks carton and feed two straws through them. The lower straw should point up toward the back of the carton.

2 Make two thin airfoils (see pages 22-23) and thread a straw through both of them. Pierce the middle of the straw with the inside of a ballpoint pen.

3 Your windmill is going to turn a cam, which will push a hammer up. Cut out the shapes shown here from stiff cardboard to make the cam, the hammer, and a table that the hammer will hit.

BLOWING FROM ALL ANGLES

Try blowing on the blades of your windmill from different angles — in front, behind, and to the side. You will find that the blades will turn quickest when you blow from the front.

BLOW FROM BEHIND

BLOW FROM THE SIDE

BLOW FROM THE FRONT

4 Tape an L-shaped piece of wire to the back of the quarter circle to make the cam. Pierce a hole in the center of the hammer, push another piece of wire through this and tape it into place. Now fold the head of the hammer over.

5 Push the inside of the ballpoint pen, which is holding the blades of your windmill, through the upper straw in the carton. Now feed the wire of the cam into the back of the pen's insides so that the cam spins with the blades.

6 Feed the hammer's wire into the lower straw. Fix some modeling clay to the head of the hammer and stick the table to the side of your windmill. Now blow on your windmill and watch the blades spin.

WHY IT WORKS

The blades of your windmill act as airfoils (see pages 22-23). As air passes over them, they create lower pressure above the curved surfaces. The higher pressure below then pushes the blade up, causing the sails to turn.

DIRECTION OF ROTATION

LIFT

FLOW OF AIR

SAIL

LOW PRESSURE ABOVE SAIL

In a Spin

What you need

Thin cardboard
Drinks straws
Modeling clay
Tape

WHILE NORMAL AIRCRAFT have fixed wings, some aircraft move their wings, spinning them around to produce lift. These aircraft, including helicopters, are called rotary-winged aircraft. Build your own rotary-winged aircraft, or whirligig, and find out how its spinning wings help it to fly.

MORE LIFT

Drop your whirligig and it will spin on its own as it falls. Now make the blades' angle steeper. You will find that the whirligig flies better.

4 *Hold the second straw between your hands with the blades uppermost. Now brush your hands together quickly to spin your whirligig and release it. Watch your whirligig spin as it flies.*

WHIRLIGIG

1 *Make two blades similar to the blades of your windmill (see pages 26-27).*

2 *Attach the straw running through the middle of the blades to another straw at a right angle using tape.*

3 *Fix a lump of modeling clay to the other end of the second straw. This will keep your whirligig upright as it flies.*

WHY IT WORKS

As the blades of your whirligig spin through the air, they act like airfoils, creating low pressure above their curved surfaces (see pages 22-23). The high pressure below the blades pushes up, slowing the fall of your whirligig.

LIFT

LOW AIR PRESSURE ABOVE THE BLADES

DIRECTION OF SPIN

HIGH AIR PRESSURE BELOW THE BLADES

FINDING OUT MORE

AIRFOIL A special shape that is designed to rise when air flows over and under it. A wing is an airfoil.

BAROMETER A device that measures changes in air pressure and is used to predict the weather.

DENSITY The heaviness of a substance for a particular volume.

EFFORTLESS FLYING

Gliders and hang gliders don't need jet or propeller engines to fly. Instead, they use rising currents of warm air, called thermals, to lift them higher into the air.

DRAG Air resistance caused by disturbances in the flow of air over an object. This force slows down moving objects.

FRICTIC A force that is created when two objects rub togethe It slows down the movement of these objects as they pass each other.

POWER LIFTER

The Mil Mi-26 Halo is the most powerful helicopter in the world today.

GRAVITY The attractive force between objects. The earth's gravity keeps us on the ground.

EARLY CHOPPER

Over five hundred years ago, the Italian artist Leonardo da Vinci sketched the world's first helicopter — but it would have been too heavy to fly!

HOVERCRAFT

vehicle that moves about on a cushion of air.

LIFT An upward force that is caused by low air pressure above surface.

PITCH The movement of an aircraft when the nose either rises or falls.

PRESSURE A force caused by the weight of the atmosphere.

ROLL The movement of an aircraft when one wing rises and the other falls.

STREAMLINED A streamlined object has a shape which helps it move through the air easily.

WIND The movement of air in the atmosphere.

WIND TUNNEL A device that is used to find out how streamlined objects are. It uses trails of smoke to see how air moves over the object's surfaces and how much drag the object creates.

YAW The movement of an aircraft when it turns either to the left or the right.

REED RAFT

In 1970, the explorer Thor Heyerdahl crossed the Atlantic Ocean in a wind-powered boat made from papyrus reeds.

INDEX